Favourite Classic Writers

By Nikki Gamble

Other titles in the series:

Favourite Classic Poets

Favourite Poets

Favourite Writers

Editor: Sarah Doughty
Designer: Tessa Barwick

Published in Great Britain in 2003 by Hodder Wayland,
an imprint of Hodder Children's Books.
This paperback edition published in 2004.

A Cataloguing record for this book is available from the British Library.

ISBN 0 7502 4286 8

Printed in China by WKT Company Limited

Hodder Children's Books
A division of Hodder Headline Limited
338 Euston Road, London NW1 3BH

Contents

Louisa May Alcott (1832–1888)

Jo March, the strong independent heroine of *Little Women,* is very like her creator, Louisa Alcott. Born in 1832 Louisa was the second of four daughters of educationist Bronson Alcott and Abigail May Alcott, who was also his teaching assistant. Bronson was a high-minded dreamer whose schemes did not earn enough money to provide for the family. As she grew up Louisa became more like her practical, hardworking mother. When she was old enough, she started working as a teacher and lady's companion to help support the family.

In 1862, during the American Civil War, Louisa became a nurse in a Washington hospital but soon fell ill with typhoid fever. The treatment for the disease was very unpleasant and left her with mercury poisoning and in poor health. She returned home to Orchard House and started writing to earn money. In 1867 she became editor for a children's magazine called *Merry's Magazine* and also started working on a 'girls' story' which was to become *Little Women*. It was a domestic family story about the four March sisters and their mother. Over 130 years after its publication *Little Women* continues to be a bestseller in Britain and the USA.

Eight Cousins

After her father's death, Rose Campbell is sent to live at 'Aunt Hill' with her six aunts and seven boy cousins! Life at 'Aunt Hill' is very different from the routines to which she has become accustomed. Will Rose be able to adapt to her new family?

Quote

"Merry Christmas, little daughters! I'm glad you began at once, and hope you will keep on. But I want to say one word before we sit down. Not far away from here lies a poor woman with a little new-born baby. Six children are huddled into one bed to keep from freezing, for they have no fire. There is nothing to eat over there, and the oldest boy came to tell me they were suffering hunger and cold. My girls will you give them your breakfast as a Christmas present?"

They were all unusually hungry, having waited nearly an hour, and for one minute no one spoke; only a minute, for Jo exclaimed impetuously:

"I'm so glad you came before we began!"

From: *Little Women* (Puffin Children's Classics, 1994. First published 1868).

Questions

Did Alcott base the March family on her own?
Yes. Louisa's older sister Anna was quiet and patient, like Meg March. Elizabeth, the third sister died young like Beth March. The youngest sister, May, was determined to become an artist, like Amy March.

Which writers did Alcott admire?
Louisa enjoyed Charlotte Yonge's *The Heir of Redclyffe*. In *Little Women* Jo reads this book while munching her way through a bag of apples.

Julia Jarman says:
'"Christmas won't be Christmas without presents." From this first line, the characters were so real. I was Jo when I read *Little Women* and the sequels. I wanted to be just like her – a good person despite all my faults, and a writer who tells the truth.'

Selected Bibliography

Books

Little Women (1868); *Good Wives* (1869 as *Little Women* part 2); *Little Men* (1871); *Jo's Boys* (1886); *Eight Cousins* (1875); *Rose in Bloom* (1876).

Audio Books

Little Women is available from the BBC Audio Collection and *Good Wives* from Chivers Audio Books.

Videos

Little Women, made in 1994 is available from Columbia Tri-Star Home Video.

weblinks

For more information about Louisa May Alcott, go to www.waylinks.co.uk/favclassicwriters

You may also enjoy books by Laura Ingalls Wilder, Ethel Turner and Susan Coolidge.

Lewis Carroll (1832–1898)

Lewis Carroll is the pseudonym of Charles Lutwidge Dodgson. Born in 1832, he was one of eleven brothers and sisters. Brought up by loving parents he had an idyllic childhood except for an unhappy period when he was sent away to Rugby school. From an early age Carroll showed a talent for writing and produced magazines for the family. After graduating from Oxford University, Carroll became a tutor there. His enjoyment of puzzles and logic can be seen in the *Alice* books. In his spare time he invented travelling games, and made wire puzzles. Carroll liked the company of children and his rooms at Oxford were full of music boxes, dolls and wind up toys, which were used to entertain his young friends.

Alice's Adventures in Wonderland
This delightfully illustrated version of Alice's adventures shows Alice as a modern rather than a Victorian child. The characters she meets include the White Rabbit, the Mad Hatter, the Cheshire Cat and the Queen of Hearts.

The heroine in *Alice's Adventures in Wonderland* was quite different from the pious and obedient heroines that were common in Victorian children's books. His inventive 'Nonsense' language was unlike any book that had been written before. But Carroll never publicly admitted that he wrote the Alice books. Letters addressed to him as Lewis Carroll were always returned unopened.

Quote

The Hatter opened his eyes very wide on hearing this; but all he said was, "why is a raven like a writing desk?"

"Come we shall have some fun now!" thought Alice. "I'm glad they've begun asking riddles – I believe I can guess that," she added aloud.

"Do you mean you think you can find out the answer to it?" said the March Hare.

"Exactly so," said Alice.

"Then you should say what you mean," the March Hare went on.

"I do," Alice hastily replied, "at least – at least I mean what I say – that's the same thing you know."

"Not the same thing a bit!" said the Hatter. "You might just as well say that 'I see what I eat' is the same thing as 'I eat what I see!'"

From *Alice's Adventures in Wonderland* (Penguin, 1994. First published 1865).

Questions

Were the *Alice* books written for a real child?
Yes. On the 4 July 1862 Lewis Carroll and his friend Robinson Duckworth took the three daughters of the Dean of Christ Church for a boating trip and picnic. They were Lorina aged 13, Alice aged ten and Edith aged eight. Carroll told them stories while rowing down the river and later Alice begged him to write them down. The heroine was named after her.

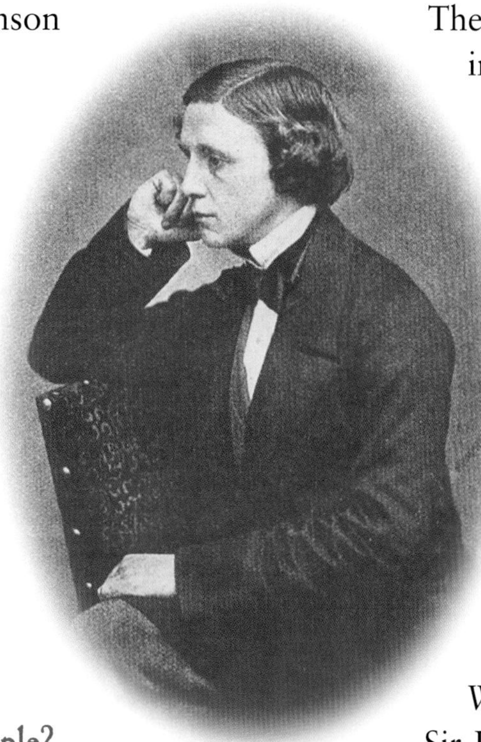

Are the characters of Wonderland based on real people?
The characters were probably based on people that the Liddell girls knew. The Mad Hatter could have been one of the Christ Church servants, Theophilus Carter, an eccentric inventor. Carroll used the names of Alice's sisters for the Eaglet and the Lory and his own name for the Dodo.

Who illustrated the *Alice* books?
Lewis Carroll drew his own pictures for his handwritten story *Alice Underground* but the first published edition of *Alice's Adventures in Wonderland* was illustrated by Sir John Tenniel. Look out for versions by Anthony Browne and Helen Oxenbury.

Selected Bibliography

Books

Alice's Adventures in Wonderland (1865); *Through the Looking Glass and What Alice Found There* (1872).

Audio Books

Alice in Wonderland and *Through the Looking Glass* (BBC Audio Collection).

Videos

Disney's animated version of *Alice in Wonderland* made in 1951 is available on video. Many films have been made of *Alice in Wonderland*. The most recent version starring Whoppi Goldberg as the Cheshire Cat is available from Warner Home Video.

weblinks

For more information about Lewis Carroll, go to www.waylinks.co.uk/favclassicwriters

You may also enjoy books by Frank L. Baum and Edward Lear.

Frances Hodgson Burnett (1849–1924)

Today, Frances Hodgson Burnett is best remembered for *The Secret Garden*, but when she was alive it was another story, *Little Lord Fauntleroy*, which captured the public imagination.

As a child Frances enjoyed reading. She especially liked poetry and Harriet Beecher Stowe's *Uncle Tom's Cabin* was one of her favourite books. She was an imaginative child who liked to make up stories, which she would act out with her collection of dolls. In 1865, when Frances was 16, the family moved from Manchester to Tennessee, USA. When her mother died five years later, Frances had to earn a living by writing short stories (as her father had also died when she was very young). She travelled frequently and had homes in America and England. She was a very popular writer in her own time and had 54 books and 13 stage plays published.

Quote

She put her hands under the leaves and began to pull and push them aside. Thick as the ivy hung, it nearly all was a loose and swinging curtain, though some had crept over wood and iron. Mary's heart began to thump and her hands to shake a little in her delight and excitement. The robin kept singing and twittering away and tilting his head on one side, as if he were as excited as she was. What was this under her hands which was square and made of iron and which her fingers found a hole in?

It was the lock of the door which had been closed ten years, and she put her hand in her pocket, drew out the key, and found it fitted the keyhole. She put the key in and turned it. It took two hands to do it, but it did turn.

From: *The Secret Garden* (Hodder Children's Books, 1994. First published 1911).

Questions

Who was Little Lord Fauntleroy?

When her son Vivian showed an interest in the English aristocracy Frances started to tell him the story of a little American boy, Cedric, who became an English Lord.

Did Burnett write stories about her own childhood?

When she lived in Manchester, Frances attended a small private school similar to the one in *A Little Princess*. Like the heroine of the story, Sara Crewe, she also entertained the other pupils with her stories.

Did the Secret Garden really exist?

The Secret Garden was inspired by three gardens. The first was Frances' garden at her home on Long Island, New York. The rose garden and the robin belonged to an earlier home, Rolveden in Kent. The third garden was one from her childhood in Salford which had, 'a little green door in the high wall that surrounded the garden.'

A Little Princess

When Sara Crewe arrives in London from India she is treated like 'a little princess' at her new school. But when her father dies, leaving her without a penny, she is forced to live in the attic with the servants.

Gillian Cross says:

'Mary Lennox is just a sulky little girl wandering round a cold winter garden – but her story is mysterious and exciting and beautiful. It made me understand that the real world is better than any fantasy, because it's where all the important things happen in our lives. That's what I try to write about too.'

Selected Bibliography

Books

Little Lord Fauntleroy (1886); *A Little Princess* (1905); *The Secret Garden* (1911); *The Lost Prince* (1915).

Audio Books

There are many versions available. *The Secret Garden* and *A Little Princess* are available on cassette from Penguin Audiobooks.

Videos

The Secret Garden (1993) and *A Little Princess* (1995) from Warner Home Video.

weblinks

For more information about Frances Hodgson Burnett, go to www.waylinks.co.uk/favclassicwriters

You may also also enjoy books by Philippa Pearce, Helen Cresswell and Edith Nesbit.

Robert Louis Stevenson (1850–1894)

Robert Louis Stevenson was born in Edinburgh in 1850. As a child he had repeated bouts of illness and spent a lot of time confined to his bed. When he was 18 months old a nurse, nicknamed Cummy, was employed to take care of him. She sang songs and psalms and read him dramatic stories from Cassell's *Illustrated Family Papers*, which probably influenced his taste for writing adventure stories.

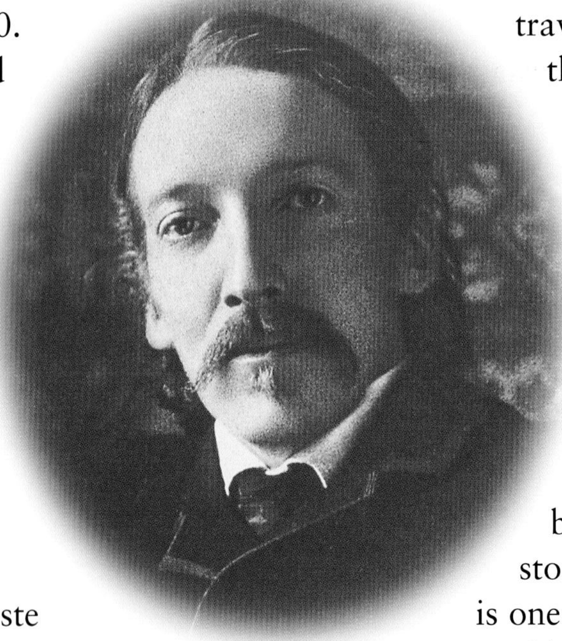

Throughout his life Stevenson suffered from bad health and nightmares. He even said that the idea for *Dr Jekyll and Mr Hyde* came from one of these bad dreams.

He spent a lot of time travelling to find a climate that would suit his health and eventually settled on the island of Samoa, which is a tropical island in the south-central part of the Pacific Ocean.

Treasure Island, Stevenson's best known book is a great adventure story and Long John Silver is one of literature's most memorable characters. Unlike most characters in Victorian children's books, it isn't obvious if Silver is a good or bad character. Although he is a villain he also looks after the fatherless cabin boy, Jim Hawkins.

Quote

In I got bodily into the apple barrel, and found there was scarce an apple left; but sitting down there in the dark, what with the sound of the waters and the rocking movement of the ship, I had either fallen asleep or was on the point of doing so, when a heavy man sat down with rather a clash close by. The barrel shook as he leaned his shoulder against it, and I was just about to jump up when the man began to speak.

It was Silver's voice, and, before I had heard a dozen words, I would not have shown myself for all the world, but lay there trembling and listening, in the extreme of fear and curiosity; for from these dozen words I understood that the lives of all the honest men aboard depended on me alone.

From: *Treasure Island* (Penguin 1994. First published 1881–82).

Questions

Was *Treasure Island* written for a particular child?

In August 1881 Stevenson was on holiday with his family. The weather was wet and miserable so to keep his young stepson Lloyd Osborne amused Stevenson drew a detailed map of an imaginary island – Treasure Island. Stories to accompany the map soon followed.

Where is Treasure Island?

Nobody knows for sure but Stevenson admitted that he took the idea for Dead Man's Chest from Charles Kingsley, whose Dead Chest Island was off the coast of Puerto Rico. Other people have suggested that it is an island off Cuba, or Unst in the Shetland Islands.

Which writers did Stevenson admire?

As a child, Stevenson enjoyed adventure stories such as R.M. Ballantyne's *Coral Island* and James Fenimore Cooper's *The Last of the Mohicans*; the influence of these writers can be seen in his own books. The adult Stevenson wrote about his admiration for authors such as Henry James, Rudyard Kipling and James Barrie.

Kidnapped

Kidnapped is a dramatic adventure set in the Scottish Highlands during the Jacobite Rebellions. The young hero David Balfour is attacked, kidnapped and the shipwrecked on a barren island.

Selected Bibliography

Books

Treasure Island (1881–82); *Kidnapped* (1886); *Dr Jekyll and Mr Hyde* (1886); *The Black Arrow* (1888).

Audio Books

There are many versions available. *Treasure Island* and *Kidnapped* are available from the BBC Audio Collection.

Videos

Five films have been made of *Treasure Island* including *Muppet Treasure Island*, made in 1996. An action packed, live action version, starring Charlton Heston as Long John Silver, is available from Warner Home Video.

weblinks

For more information about Robert Louis Stevenson, go to www.waylinks.co.uk/favclassicwriters

You may also enjoy books by Walter Scott, R.M. Ballantyne and Rider Hagard.

Edith Nesbit (1858–1924)

Edith Nesbit was born in London, the youngest of five children. When she was three her father died and Edith moved to France with her mother and sisters. The long summer holidays the family spent at La Haye, Brittany, later provided inspiration for the adventures of the Bastable children in her books. Edith returned to England when she was 13 years old.

When she was 20 Edith married and became very interested in politics. She became a member of the Fabian Society.

In 1898, she wrote a series of stories about Oswald Bastable and his brothers and sisters for several magazines. The stories were later published as books and called *The Story of the Treasure Seekers*. After this, she produced many books for children including the well-loved *Five Children and It* and *The Railway Children*.

When she died in 1924 Nesbit had written 44 novels, mostly for children. She was a great influence on the writers who followed her and she is credited with inventing the adventure story for children.

Quote

"Stand firm," said Peter, "and wave like mad! When it gets to the big furze bush step back, but go on waving! Don't stand *on* the line Bobbie!"

The train came rattling along very, very fast.

"They don't see us! They won't see us! It's all no good!" cried Bobbie.

The two little flags on the line swayed as the nearing train shook and loosened the heaps of loose stones that held them up. One of them slowly leaned over and fell on the line. Bobbie jumped forward and caught it up, and waved it; her hands did not tremble now.

It seemed that the train came on as fast as ever. It was very near now.

"Keep off the line, you silly cuckoo!" said Peter, fiercely.

"It's no good," Bobbie said again.

"Stand back!" cried Peter suddenly, and he dragged Phyllis back by the arm.

But Bobbie cried, "Not yet, not yet!" and waved her two flags right over the line. The front of the engine looked black and enormous. Its voice was loud and harsh.

"Oh stop, stop, stop!" cried Bobbie.

From: *The Railway Children* (Puffin, 1995. First published 1906).

Questions

Did Nesbit base her children's stories on her own childhood?

The Bastable children were very much like Edith's own brothers and sisters. The twins Alice and Noel were most like Edith herself. On one occasion the children thought that Edith looked so pretty that she ought to be planted like a flower. Edith recalls this incident in *The Story of the Treasure Seekers* in the episode where the Bastables bury Albert-next-door in the garden.

Where did Nesbit get the idea for the dinosaur park in *The Enchanted Castle*?

In 1854 Queen Victoria and Prince Albert opened a dinosaur park at Crystal Palace. The giant sculptures built by Benjamin Waterhouse Hawkins were quite a spectacle and can still be visited today. In Edith's magical story the stone dinosaurs come to life after dark.

Who was influenced by Nesbit's writing?

C.S. Lewis was a great admirer of Edith's stories.

The Story of the Treasure Seekers

When the Bastable family falls on hard times, the children think up a series of ingenious schemes to help their father and restore their fortune.

Selected Bibliography

Books

The Story of the Treasure Seekers (1899); *The Book of Dragons* (1899); *The Wouldbegoods* (1901); *Five Children and It* (1902); *The Phoenix and the Carpet* (1904); *The Story of the Amulet* (1906); *The Railway Children* (1906); *Enchanted Castle* (1907); *The House of Arden* (1908).

Audio Books

Versions of *The Railway Children* are available on audio-cassette from Penguin Audio Books and BBC Audio. *The Phoenix and the Carpet* is available from Chivers Children's Audio Books.

Videos

Films of *The Railway Children* are available from Warner Home Video and Carlton Home Entertainment. *The Treasure Seekers* is also available on video from Carlton Home Entertainment. *Five Children and It* was made into a television serial and is available from BBC Worldwide Videos.

weblinks

For more information about Edith Nesbit, go to www.waylinks.co.uk/favclassicwriters

You may also enjoy books by C.S. Lewis, Lucy Boston and Sylvia Waugh.

Kenneth Grahame (1859–1932)

Kenneth Grahame first found fame with his books for adults but today he is remembered for *The Wind in the Willows*, the adventures of Mole, Rat, Badger and Toad.

Grahame was born in Edinburgh but when he was just four years old his mother died and he was sent to live with his grandmother in Cookham Dean, a village on the river Thames in Berkshire. Grahame loved it near the river that was to be his inspiration for *The Wind in the Willows*. He would often spend solitary days wandering along its banks. When he was nine years old he was sent to boarding school in Oxford where a favourite pastime was canoeing on the River Thames.

Grahame hoped to go to Oxford University but his uncle refused to support his studies so he became a clerk in a bank instead. Work at the bank was quite relaxed and Grahame found plenty of time to write books. He met and married Elspeth Thompson and they had one son Alastair whom they nicknamed 'Mouse'.

The Reluctant Dragon
'I can't fight and I won't fight' the dragon announces. But the townsfolk insist that he must do battle with St. George.

Quote

The Badger drew himself up, took a firm grip of his stick with both paws, glanced round at his comrades and cried:

"The hour is come! Follow me!"

And flung the door open wide.

My! What a squealing and squeaking and a screeching filled the air!

Well might the terrified weasels dive under the tables and spring madly up at the windows! Well might the ferrets rush wildly for the fire-place and get hopelessly jammed in the chimney! Well might the tables and chairs be upset, and glass and china be sent crashing on the floor, in the panic of that terrible moment when the four Heroes strode wrathfully into the room!

From: *The Wind in the Willows* (Pavilion Books, 2001. First published 1908).

Questions

How did *The Wind in the Willows* come to be written?

The Wind in the Willows started as bed-time stories to soothe Alastair's tantrums. Grahame said 'Alastair had a bad crying fit. I told him stories about moles, giraffes and water-rats to calm him down.'

Who illustrated *The Wind in the Willows*?

The most famous illustrations were produced in 1930 by E.H. Shepard. Since then there have been many illustrated versions. Look out for copies illustrated by Inga More, Rene Cloke, John Burningham and Michael Foreman.

Melvin Burgess says:
'*The Wind in the Willows* was the very first book I fell in love with – I must have read my favourite parts dozens of times by the time I was eight. For me it wasn't Toad who appealed – it was Ratty and Mole. What I love about it is the love of place, of home and of the details that make up so much of the real quality of life. Certainly in my own writing, however different, I always want that strong physical sense of place to come through.'

Selected Bibliography

Books

The Reluctant Dragon (1898); *The Wind in the Willows* (1908).

Audio Books

The Wind in the Willows and *The Reluctant Dragon* are available on cassette from BBC Audio Collection.

Videos

There have been many different film versions of *The Wind in the Willows*. An animated version made in 1983 is available from P.T. Video.

On the stage

A.A. Milne adapted *The Wind in the Willows* for his play *The Toad of Toad Hall*. Alan Bennett also adapted Grahame's book for the National Theatre. The Theatre Museum in London displays costumes from the National Theatre production.

weblinks

For more information about Kenneth Grahame, go to www.waylinks.co.uk/favclassicwriters

You may also enjoy books by Brian Jacques, Colin Dann or Gary Kilworth.

Rudyard Kipling (1865–1936)

Joseph Rudyard Kipling was born in Bombay, India where his father was the principal of the new Art School. At six years old he was sent to live with foster parents in England because the Indian climate was believed to be unhealthy for British children. He was treated cruelly and after six unhappy years he was sent away to boarding school. At first he disliked the school but he soon grew accustomed to the tough routines. The school was immortalized in the schoolboy exploits, *Stalky and Co.*

Kipling showed an interest in writing from an early age. He wrote verse and became editor of the school magazine. His headmaster told his parents, 'You must not be too hopeful of his sticking to any profession but literature.' After leaving school Kipling returned to India to work as a journalist on the *Lahore Gazette*. He drew on his experience of India and knowledge of its folklore to write the *Jungle Books* and *Kim*.

Quote

This, O Best Beloved, is another story of the High and Far-Off Times. In the very middle of those times was a Stickly-Prickly Hedgehog, and he lived on the banks of the turbid Amazon, eating shelly snails and things. And he had a friend, a Slow-Solid Tortoise, who lived on the banks of the turbid Amazon, eating green lettuce and things. And so *that* was all right, Best Beloved. Do you see?

But also, and at the same time, in those High and Far Off Times, there was a Painted Jaguar, and he lived on the banks of the turbid Amazon too; and he ate everything that he could catch. When he could not catch deer or monkeys he would eat frogs and beetles; and when he could not catch frogs and beetles he went to his Mother Jaguar, and she told him how to eat hedgehogs and tortoises.

From: *Just So Stories* (Penguin, 1994. First published 1902).

Questions

How did the *Just So Stories* get its title?

The *Just So Stories* started out as bedtime stories for Kipling's daughter 'Effie' and she always insisted that they should be told 'just so'. These were originally published as separate stories. Then around 1901 Kipling decided to collect them together to make one book and he used Effie's words for the title.

The Jungle Book

When a human baby is left alone, abandoned in the jungle, a family of wolves raise him and protect him from the man-eating tiger, Shere Khan. Bagheera, the black panther, and Baloo, the bear, take charge of his education.

Susan Price says:

'I revelled in the language of the *Just So Stories*, with their 'O Best Beloved', and their rhythmical, almost chanting cadences. 'The Sing-Song of Old Man Kangaroo' particularly stays in my memory. I think these chanting rhythms surfaced in my *Ghost World* trilogy. Though my books are different in tone from the *Just So Stories*, Kipling showed me what could be done with words.'

Who illustrated the *Just So Stories*?

Kipling produced his own pen and ink drawings, which were used when the book was first published.

Did Kipling receive any honours for his writing?

Yes, Kipling was presented with the most prestigious award, the Nobel Prize for Literature, in 1907.

Selected Bibliography

Books

The Jungle Book (1894); *The Second Jungle Book* (1895); *Just So Stories* (1902); *Puck of Pook's Hill* (1907); *Rewards and Fairies* (1910).

Audio Books

The Jungle Book and *Just So Stories* are available as Penguin Audio Books.

Videos

The Jungle Book has inspired two Walt Disney films. An animated version was made in 1967 and a live action film in 1994. Both are available on home video.

You may also enjoy Ted Hughes' *How the Whale Became* and Rosemary Sutcliff's *Warrior Scarlet*.

Arthur Ransome (1884–1967)

Arthur Ransome was born and grew up in Leeds. His happiest childhood memories were the annual family holidays in the Lake District. Ransome was a keen reader. One of his favourite books, *Holiday House* by Catherine Sinclair, is about a group of children enjoying the freedom of their holidays. This was something that Ransome later wrote about in his own books. After leaving school Ransome worked as an office boy for a publishing company and started his writing career by placing stories and articles in newspapers. In 1903 he gave up his job so that he could concentrate on the writing. Ransome is best remembered for the 12 books in his sailing adventure series *Swallows and Amazons*, which had a big influence on the writers that came after him. The holiday story became a firmly established favourite for the next thirty years. 1n 1936 he was the first writer to receive the Carnegie Medal for his novel, *Pigeon Post*.

Peter Duck

John, Susan, Titty and Roger sail with Captain Flint and Peter Duck in search of buried pirate treasure. Their adventure takes them into many dangers and they must fight a villainous band of pirates before winning their prize.

Quote

Slowly Swallow moved in among rocks awash. Then, besides the rocks awash, there were rocks showing above water. These grew bigger. Then there were high rocks that hid the eastern side of the lake, while the western side was hidden by a long rocky point sticking out from the island. It was almost like being between two walls. Remembering what he had seen when he climbed out on the big rock above the pool, John kept Swallow as near as he could to the eastern wall, Titty with her oar fending off when the rock seemed too close. If they had been rowing in the ordinary way their oars would have touched the rocks on either side. Still Swallow moved on with the water clear under her keel.

From: *Swallows and Amazons* (Red Fox, Random House 1993. First published 1930).

Questions

Where did Ransome get the idea for *Swallows and Amazons*?

Ransome was often asked this question and here is the answer he gave: '. . . as children, my brother, my sisters and I spent most of our holidays on a farm at the south end of Coniston. We played in or on the lake or on the hills above it, finding friends in the farmers and shepherds and charcoal-burners. *Swallows and Amazons* grew out of those old memories.'

Did Ransome write any stories other than the *Swallows and Amazons* series?

Ransome lived for a while in Russia. During his stay there he became very interested in Russian folklore. In 1917 he published a collection of stories called *Old Peter's Russian Tales*.

Tim Bowler says:

'Arthur Ransome's fictional landscapes (or rather seascapes) dominated my childhood and still echo through my life. I was utterly absorbed into his world and sometimes even used to read his books while out sailing with my parents. I'd make an excuse to go down to the cabin, pull out *Peter Duck* or *Swallowdale* or whatever, and dive into it. Ransome's genius had made fictional sailing even more compelling than the real thing.'

Selected Bibliography

Books

Swallows and Amazons (1930); *Swallowdale* (1931); *Peter Duck* (1932); *Winter Holiday* (1933); *Coot Club* (1934) *Pigeon Post* (1936), *We Didn't Mean to Go to Sea* (1937); *Missee Lee* (1941) *Great Northern* (1947).

Audio Books

Swallows and Amazons is available on cassette from Isis Audio Books.

Videos

A film of *Swallows and Amazons* is available on Warner Home Video.

weblinks

For more information about Arthur Ransome, go to www.waylinks.co.uk/favclassicwriters

You may also enjoy books by Malcolm Saville or Willard Price.

Richmal Crompton (1890–1969)

Richmal Crompton Lamburn was born on 15 November 1890 in Bury, Lancashire. She trained to be a classics teacher and became classics mistress at Bromley High School in Kent. After a severe attack of polio in 1923 she was forced to give up teaching and became a full-time writer.

Richmal was the author of 38 books about the mischievous schoolboy, William Brown, who first appeared in a story called *The Rice Mould* published in *Home Magazine* in 1919. In the stories, William and his loyal gang the *Outlaws* always manage to triumph over the despairing adults. Although William remained 11 years old throughout the series, some things did change. In the first books William lived in a very large house with stables, summerhouses and lots of servants but in the later books his home is fairly ordinary; the vicarage tea parties disappear and television is introduced.

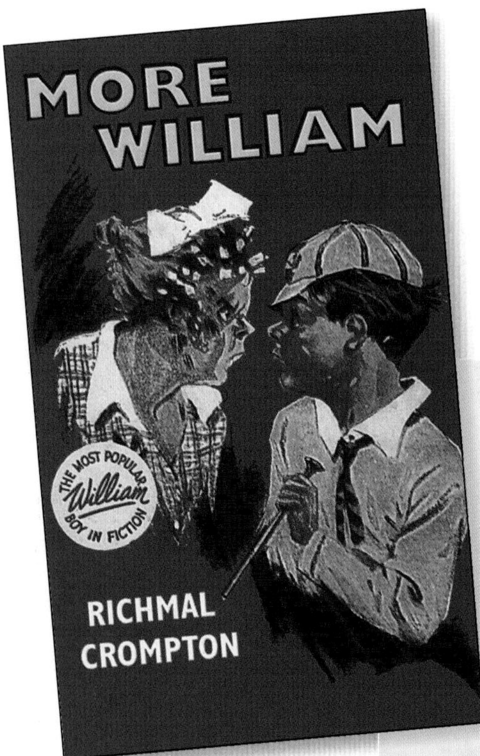

More William
Who's to blame when a centipede appears on Aunt Evangeline's plate? William, of course. This book includes fourteen hilarious stories about the mischievous William Brown.

Quote

Just as Robert was taking up a plate of sandwiches to hand them with a courteous gesture to Miss Cannon, his eyes fell upon the long, white road leading from the village to the riverside and remained fixed there, his face frozen with horror. The hand that held the plate dropped listlessly back again on to the tablecloth. Their eyes followed his. A curious figure was cycling along the road – a figure with a blackened face and a few drooping feathers on its head, and a doormat flying in the wing. A crowd of small children ran behind cheering. It was a figure vaguely familiar to them all.

"It can't be," said Robert hoarsely, passing a hand over his brow.

No one spoke.

It came nearer and nearer. There was no mistaking it.

"William!" gasped four voices.

From: *Just William* (Macmillan 1991. First published 1922).

Questions

Has a film ever been made of the *William* stories?

Several versions have been made for the cinema and television. The first film, called *Just William*, was made in 1939. The most recent television series was made by the BBC in 1994.

Was the character of *William* based on anyone that Crompton knew?

Yes, she drew inspiration for William from the childhood exploits of her brother Jack.

Who illustrated the *William* books?

The first books were illustrated by Thomas Henry Fisher in the early 1920s but he didn't meet Richmal until 1958.

> Morris Gleitzman says:
> 'As a younger man I couldn't get enough of the wonderful William. Not only was he the messiest character I'd ever read, but he was the most passionate too. William's problems were never trivial – not to him. Those are the kinds of stories I like to write – young people grappling with the biggest problem in their lives at that moment. I think there's a bit of William in most of my characters. There's still a lot of *William* on my bookshelves.'

Selected Bibliography

Books

Just William (1922); *More William* (1922); *William Again* (1923); *William the Fourth* (1924); *Still William* (1925); *William the Conqueror* (1926).

Audio Books

Audio Books of the William stories are available from the BBC Audio Collection. The stories are narrated by Martin Jarvis.

weblinks

For more information about Richmal Crompton, go to www.waylinks.co.uk/favclassicwriters

You may also enjoy books by Anthony Buckridge, Morris Gleitzman and Paul Jennings.

J.R.R. Tolkien (1892–1973)

John Ronald Reuel Tolkien was born on 3 January 1892 at Bloemfontein in South Africa. His health was badly affected by the hot climate and so his mother returned to England in 1895 with her two sons while his father remained in South Africa. Tolkien was never to see him again as he died soon after.

At school Tolkien had a particular gift for languages, fostered by his mother. He studied Latin, Greek and Old and Middle English. Then he started to invent his own languages for 'elvish' people to use. His love of words is evident in his writing.

At 19 years old, Tolkien won a scholarship to Oxford University, gained a First in English and became a tutor at the university, like his friend C.S. Lewis.

Tolkien's ambition was to create a mythology for English literature. His first step to achieving this was *The Silmarillion*, a collection of stories about the creation of Middle-Earth. It tells of the three great elf jewels stolen by the evil power Morgoth and the wars fought to win them back. For his children he wrote *The Hobbit* and *The Lord of the Rings*, which took 12 years to complete.

The Hobbit

Home-loving hobbit Bilbo is content with his life until Gandalf the wizard arrives with a band of dwarves. Suddenly he is thrust unwillingly into a dangerous quest which leads to the treasure hoard of Smaug the Magnificent, a terrifying dragon.

Quote

The Balrog reached the bridge. Gandalf stood in the middle of the span. Leaning on his staff in his left hand, but in the other hand Glamdring gleamed, cold and white. His enemy halted again, facing him, and the shadow about it reached out like two vast wings. It raised the whip, and the thongs whined and cracked. Fire came from its nostrils but Gandalf stood firm.

"You cannot pass," he said. The orcs stood still, and a dead silence fell. "I am a servant of the Secret Fire, wielder of the flame of Anor. You cannot pass. The dark fire will not avail you, flame of Udûn. Go back to the Shadow! You cannot pass."

From: *The Lord of the Rings* (Collins, 1995. First published 1954).

Questions

What books did Tolkien enjoy reading when he was a child?

Alice's Adventures in Wonderland, the *Curdie* stories by George Macdonald, *Arthurian Legend* and Andrew Lang's colour fairy books especially the legend of *Sigurd and the Dragon Fafnir*.

Did Tolkien write about people he knew in his stories?

There is a remarkable likeness between Bilbo Baggins and his creator, including their love of bright waistcoats. Tolkien once wrote, 'I am in fact a hobbit in all but size.'

Who illustrated *The Hobbit*?

Tolkien drew the illustrations himself.

Is Middle-Earth based on a real place?

Parts of Middle-Earth are recognizable as places that Tolkien knew. With its mill and river, Hobbiton is Sarehole in Warwickshire (now West Midlands) where Tolkien lived when he was a child.

Selected Bibliography

Books

The Hobbit (1937); *The Lord of the Rings* (1954, 1955); *The Father Christmas Letters* (1976); *The Silmarillion* (1977).

Audio Books

The Lord of the Rings and *The Hobbit* are available from the BBC Audio Collection. An audio version of *The Silmarillion* is available from HarperCollins.

Videos

The Lord of the Rings has inspired two films. The 1978 version is available from Warner Home Video. The 2002 version of the first part of the book is available on DVD. An interesting film about the landscapes that inspired Tolkien's Middle-Earth called *Beyond the Movie – Lord of Rings* has been produced by the National Geographic Society.

weblinks

For more information about J.R.R Tolkien, go to www.waylinks.co.uk/favclassicwriters

You may also enjoy books by Ursula le Guin, Terry Pratchett and Lloyd Alexander.

C.S. Lewis (1898–1963)

Clive Staple Lewis was born in Belfast in 1898. As a child, he enjoyed reading, especially Beatrix Potter. One of his earliest books was *Squirrel Nutkin* and like Beatrix Potter, Lewis also liked to draw animals dressed as humans.

When he was just nine years old Lewis's mother died and he was sent away to boarding school with his older brother, Warren. He hated the school and wrote to his father begging to be allowed home. After the First World War (1914–18) Lewis gained a classics degree from Oxford University. In 1925 he became a tutor there and developed a great friendship with J.R.R. Tolkien. They met for weekly chats about their writing. Lewis admired Tolkien's *Lord of the Rings*, but sadly Tolkien didn't think very much of Lewis's *Narnia Chronicles*.

Quote

Next moment she found that what was rubbing against her face and hands was no longer soft fur but something hard and rough and even prickly. "Why, it is just like branches of trees!" exclaimed Lucy. And then she saw that there was a light ahead of her; not a few inches away where the back of the wardrobe ought to have been, but a long way off. Something cold and soft was falling on her. A moment later she found that she was standing in the middle of a wood at night-time with snow under her feet and snowflakes falling through the air.

From: *The Lion, the Witch and the Wardrobe* (HarperCollins, 2001. First published 1950).

The Lion, the Witch and the Wardrobe

Through the wardrobe, Lucy stumbles on a wonderful land of fauns and cantaurs, nymphs and talking animals. But the land is ruled by a cruel White Witch, and can only be freed by Aslan the Lion, and the four children.

Questions

Who illustrated Lewis's books?
The original illustrator, Pauline Baynes, was introduced to Lewis by Tolkien.

Did Lewis's childhood play any part in his books?
In 1905 the Lewis family moved to Little Lea, a big rambling house which was the inspiration for the professor's house in *The Lion, the Witch and the Wardrobe.*

Did Lewis win any awards for his books?
Yes, he was awarded the Carnegie Medal for *The Last Battle* in 1956.

Were Lewis's books adapted in any other ways?
A opera based on the Chronicles of Narnia, was written in 1969. *The Lion, The Witch and the Wardrobe* was most recently adapted by Adrian Mitchell for the Royal Shakespeare Company

Jenny Nimmo says:
'I was eight years old and reading was my way of entering the world of make-believe. Snow had always seemed different and magical and when I read the part in *The Lion, the Witch and the Wardrobe* where Lucy enters Narnia for the first time I felt had never read anything more wonderful. Immediately, I became Lucy and stepped out of the world I knew into a place where something marvellous and astonishing was going to happen.'

Selected Bibliography

Books

The Lion, the Witch and the Wardrobe (1950); Prince Caspian (1951); *The Voyage of the Dawn Treader* (1952); *The Silver Chair* (1953); *A Horse and His Boy* (1954); *The Magician's Nephew* (1955); *The Last Battle* (1956).

Audio Books

The Chronicles of Narnia are all available as audio books from the BBC Radio Collection.

Videos

The Lion, the Witch and the Wardrobe, Prince Caspian, The Voyage of the Dawn Treader and *The Silver Chair* are available from the BBC Worldwide Publishing.

weblinks
For more information about C.S. Lewis, go to www.waylinks.co.uk/favclassicwriters

You may also enjoy books by J.K. Rowling, Diana Wynne Jones and Susan Cooper.

E.B. White (1899–1985)

White received many letters from children who had read his books. They often asked him questions about his writing such as how old he was when he started to write. He answered; "I can't remember any time in my life when I wasn't busy writing . . . I think children often find pleasure and satisfaction in trying to set their thoughts down on paper, either in words or in pictures. I was no good at drawing, so I used words instead. As I grew older, I found that writing can be a way of earning a living . . . "

Elwyn Brooks White is the author of *Charlotte's Web*, the heart-warming story about Wilbur the pig and his devoted friend Charlotte, a spider who can spell. He was also a very successful journalist and also wrote 20 books of prose and poetry.

White was born in New York in 1899. He was a very shy child who grew into a shy adult but he was also very witty and good-humoured. After leaving school he went on to study at Cornell University where he worked on the college newspaper. White was very concerned about environmental issues and he campaigned against the H-bomb and pollution.

Quote

At last Wilbur saw the creature that had spoken to him in such a kindly way. Stretched across the upper part of the doorway was a big spider's web, and hanging from the top of the web, head down, was a large grey spider. She was about the size of a gumdrop. She had eight legs, and she was waving one of them at Wilbur in friendly greeting. "See me now?" she asked."Oh yes indeed," said Wilbur. " Yes indeed! How are you? Good morning! Salutations! Very pleased to meet you. What is your name please? May I have you name?"

"My name," said the spider, "is Charlotte."

"Charlotte what?" asked Wilbur, eagerly.

"Charlotte A. Cavatica. But just call me Charlotte."

From: *Charlotte's Web* (Puffin Modern Classics, 1993. First published 1952).

Questions

Where did the ideas for White's stories come from?

By the time he started writing books for children, White had retired to the country. He had a farm in Maine and while he lived there he took a great interest in the animals. Some of the animals have found their way into his books.

Did White receive any awards for his stories?

Yes, in 1970 he was presented with the American Library Association's Laura Ingalls Wilder Medal in recognition for his long-lasting contribution to children's literature. In 1971 he was also honoured for his writing for adults with the National Medal for Literature.

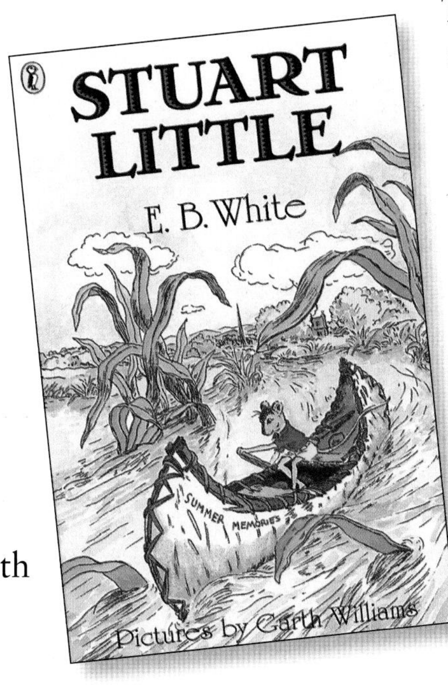

Did White write his stories for one particular child?

Yes, he started to write *Stuart Little* to keep his six-year old niece entertained, but by the time the book was completed she had grown up!

Who illustrated White's books?

The original illustrations for *Charlotte's Web* and *Stuart Little* were drawn by Garth Williams who also illustrated Laura Ingalls Wilder's *Little House on the Prairie*. Eight other illustrators had been tried first!

Stuart Little

Stuart Little lives in New York with his parents, his older brother George, and Snowball the cat. But there's one extraordinary thing about Stuart – he is a MOUSE!

Selected Bibliography

Books

Stuart Little (1945); *Charlotte's Web* (1952); *The Trumpet of the Swan* (1970).

Videos

An animated film of *Charlotte's Web* was made in 1973 and is available from Mia Video Entertainment. The 1999 film of *Stuart Little* is available on video from Columbia Tri-Star Home Video and *Stuart Little 2* has also been released.

Audio Books

Stuart Little, *Charlotte's Web* and *The Trumpet of the Swan* are available on CD from the Listening Library.

weblinks

For more information about E.B. White, go to www.waylinks.co.uk/favclassicwriters

You may also enjoy books by Dick King-Smith or Dodie Smith.

Tove Jansson (1914–2001)

Moomins are loveable hippopotamus-like creatures that live in idyllic Moominvalley. They hibernate through the cold Finnish winters but when spring comes they are ready for adventure.

The Moomins' creator, Swedish speaking Finn Tove Jansson, was born in Helsinki in 1914. Her mother was an illustrator and her father a sculptor so it is not surprising that she developed a talent for drawing. The family spent the winters in the city and summers on a small island in the Gulf of Finland, which Jansson used as the setting for the Moomin books. The Moomins first appeared in Britain in a book called *Finn Family Moomintroll*. In 1954 Jansson started to illustrate a strip cartoon of the Moomins for the *London Evening News* which secured her popularity in Britain. Between 1945–77 she wrote 13 Moomin books which were translated into thirty languages.

Comet in Moominland

A comet is speeding towards the Earth and nobody knows what to do about it. So Moomintroll sets out to see if he can prevent a catastrophe. *Comet in Moominland* was the second Moomin book to be published in Finland in 1946.

Quote

One grey morning the first snow began to fall in the Valley of the Moomins. It fell softly and quietly, and in a few hours everything was white.

Moomintroll stood on his doorstep and watched the valley nestle beneath its winter blanket. "Tonight," he thought, "we shall settle down for our long winter's sleep." (All Moomintrolls go to sleep about November. This is a good idea, too, if you don't like the cold and long winter darkness.) Shutting the door behind him, Moomintroll stole in to his mother and said:

"The snow has come!"

From: *Finn Family Moomintroll* (Puffin Books, 1961. First published in English in 1950).

Questions

Are the Moomins based on Jansson's family?
They have some similar characteristics. Jansson's mother, like Moominmama, enjoyed looking after her home, picking mushrooms, bottling fruit and taking care of her children. Her father was more of a dreamer, like Moominpapa.

Where is Moominvalley?
With its thick forests and archipelagos, Moominvalley is typical of the Finnish landscape. Life in Moominvalley is seasonal and the emotions of the characters are affected by the changes in the seasons.

Philip Pullman says:
'Tove Jansson's Moomins are some of the most mysterious of invented beings. Such is her strange power that they don't seem to be invented at all, however; if you have known them in your childhood, they seem to be your own family, their eccentricities and the delights and dangers of their world to be part of yours. She draws their tubby bodies, expressing so much presence with a single unshaded line, conveying so much wisdom with a simple narrative. The word that sums this up is genius, and she had it from the very first book she wrote.'

Selected Bibliography

Books (first published in English):

Finn Family Moomintroll (1950); *Comet in Moominland* (1951); *Tales from Moominvalley* (1964); *Moominpapa at Sea* (1967); *Moominvalley in November* (1971).

Audio Books

Finn Family Moomintroll is available as an audio book from BBC Audio Collection, narrated by Hugh Lawrie.

Videos

A collection of animated stories is available on a video called *Moomin Mania* from Maverick Entertainment.

weblinks
For more information about Tove Jansson, go to www.waylinks.co.uk/favclassicwriters

You may also enjoy some folk tales from Finland such as Aaron Shepard's *The Maiden of the Northland.*

Other favourite classic writers

There are so many excellent classic writers for you to get to know. Here are a few more introductions. Have a look for their stories in your public library or bookshop.

Hans Christian Andersen (1805–75)

Danish writer Hans Andersen created over 150 fairy tales such as *The Princess and the Pea, The Little Mermaid, The Ugly Duckling* and *The Emperor's New Clothes*. Born and brought up in the city of Odense, he was the only son of a shoemaker and had a very humble upbringing. But his father loved literature and would often read his son traditional stories from *The Arabian Nights* and *The Fables of La Fontaine*. The influence of these tales can be seen in some of Andersen's own stories such as *The Flying Trunk*. When you read a good translation of an Andersen story you can hear the voice of the storyteller. Today, Andersen's skilful storytelling and irony is appreciated but in his own day he was criticized for using everyday language rather than a grand, elegant style. Andersen influenced many writers including the Irish writer Oscar Wilde. His name has been given to the most prestigious international award for children's literature, the Hans Andersen Medal.

L. Frank Baum (1856–1919)

L. Frank Baum was born on 15 May 1856 in Chittenago, New York. He was a poorly child, who spent a lot of his time reading. When he was a teenager he set up his own newspaper and magazine and later became interested in the theatre. He started to tell stories to amuse his four sons. His first children's book *Mother Goose in Prose* was published in 1897 and this was followed in 1899 by *Father Goose, His Book*, which was the biggest selling children's book of the year. In 1900 the first in the series of Oz books *The Wonderful Wizard of Oz* was published. The last one *Glinda in the Land of Oz* was published after Baum's death. Several films have been made of *The Wizard of Oz*. The 1939 film starring Judy Garland as Dorothy is a classic in its own right.

Astrid Lindgren (1907–2002)

Astrid Lindgren was born Anna Emilia Ericcson in 1907 in the small Swedish town of Vimmerby. Today there is a theme park near the town called Astrid Lindgren World which children can visit to find out more about her books. Her most famous creation was Pippi Longstocking, the strongest girl in the world. The first Pippi book started as a story for Lindgren's daughter, Karin who invented the heroine's name. Astrid was the most widely read Swedish author of her time. She wrote over 100 books that have been translated into more than 60 languages.

In 1958 she was awarded the prestigious Hans Andersen Medal an international award for her important and lasting contribution to children's literature.

Rosemary Sutcliff (1920–1993)

Rosemary Sutcliff was one of the finest writers of historical fiction for young people. Her father was a naval officer so her early childhood was spent travelling. Rosemary was artistically talented and at the age of 14 she was sent to art school to train as a painter. Her first book was a retelling of the Robin Hood legend based on the old ballads. In 1954 she wrote *Eagle of the Ninth*, the first of her Roman Trilogy which was followed by *The Silver Branch* (1957) and *The Lantern Bearers* (1959). *Warrior Scarlet* (1958) is set on the Sussex Downs during the Bronze Age tells the story of a boy with a withered arm and his determination to be accepted as a warrior by his tribe. Rosemary has also written about the stories of King Arthur and Odysseus. She was interested in exploring 'the shadows and the half-lights and the echoes' that lie behind the legends.

Arthur Conan Doyle (1859–1930)

Arthur Conan Doyle, creator of the world's most famous detective Sherlock Holmes, was born in Edinburgh. In 1876–1881 while he was studying medicine he met Dr Joseph Bell and was impressed by his amazing powers of deducing his patients' history. Bell provided Conan Doyle with the idea for Sherlock Holmes who first appeared in 1887 in a short story called *A Study in Scarlet*. The detective was extremely popular with the Victorians and they were shocked in 1893 when Conan Doyle 'killed him off'. He fell to his death at the Reichenbach Falls after a struggle with his adversary Professor Moriarty. Conan Doyle also wrote historical novels, horror stories and tales of the supernatural.

W.E. Johns (1893–1968)

During World War I (1914–18), William Earle Johns joined the Royal Flying Corps. While on a mission he was shot down over Mannheim by the famous German flying ace Ernst Udet and remained a prisoner until the end of the war. Johns wrote 98 books published between 1932 and 1999 about his famous hero flying-ace James Bigglesworth. Biggles started out was a pilot with the Royal Flying Corps but in later books set in World War II (1939–45) he became squadron leader of 666 Spitfire. There are some stories set after the war in which Biggles joins Scotland Yard Flying Police Squad. Johns also wrote ten books about Worrals a female air pilot with the Women's Auxiliary Air Force (WAAF) which were first published in *Girls Own Paper* and ten books featuring Gimlet, an army commando.

Acknowledgements

The Publishers would like to thank the following publishers and illustrators who allowed us to use material in this book.

Extracts

From *The Wind in the Willows* extract by Kenneth Grahame copyright © The University Chest, Oxford, reproduced by permission of Curtis Brown Ltd., London.

From *Just So Stories* by Rudyard Kipling (Puffin, 1994). Copyright © Rudyard Kipling, 1902.

From *Swallows and Amazons* by Arthur Ransome, published by Jonathan Cape/Red Fox. Reprinted with permission of The Random House Group Ltd.

From *Just William* text copyright © Richmal C. Ashbee. This extract reproduced by permission of Macmillan Children's Books, London.

The Lord of the Rings extract reprinted by permission of HarperCollins Publishers Ltd, copyright © J.R.R. Tolkien, 1954/55.

The Lion, the Witch and the Wardrobe by C.S. Lewis, copyright © C.S. Lewis Pte. Ltd. 1950. Extract reprinted with permission.

Charlotte's Web by E.B. White (Hamish Hamilton, 1952). Copyright © 1952 by J.White.

Finn Family Moomintroll by Tove Jansson (A & C Black, 1950). Copyright © 1950 by Tove Jansson.

Jackets and illustrations

Front cover from *Eight Cousins* by Louisa M. Alcott (Puffin, 1996).

Front cover illustration © 1999 Helen Oxenbury. Reproduced from Helen Oxenbury's portrayal of *Alice's Adventures in Wonderland* by permission of Walker Books Ltd. Also reproduced on the *cover*.

Front cover from *A Little Princess* by Frances Hodgson Burnett (Puffin, 1994). Cover illustration by George Smith.

Front cover from *Kidnapped* by Robert Louis Stevenson (Puffin, 1994) and Christie's Images for permission to reproduce the painting by Alexander Nasmyth.

Front cover from *The Story of the Treasure Seekers* by E. Nesbit (Puffin, 1994). Cover illustration by Paul Finn.

Front cover illustration from *The Reluctant Dragon* copyright © 1938 E.H. Shepard, reproduced by permission of Curtis Brown Ltd., London.

Illustrations copyright © 1996 Inga Moore from *The River Bank and Other Stories From the Wind in the Willows*. Written by Kenneth Grahame. Reproduced by permission of the publisher Walker Books Ltd., London. Also used on the *title page*.

Front cover from *The Jungle Book* by Rudyard Kipling (Puffin, 1994). Cover illustration by Sally Taylor.

Front cover from *Peter Duck* by Arthur Ransome reprinted by permission of The Random House Group, Ltd.

Front cover illustration from *More William* by Thomas Henry Fisher. Copyright © Thomas Henry Fisher Estate. Reproduced by permission of Macmillan Children's Books, London. Also reproduced on the *cover*.

Front cover from *The Hobbit*: reprinted by permission of HarperCollins Publishers Ltd, copyright © J.R.R. Tolkien, 1937. Also reproduced on the *cover*.

Cover illustrations by Pauline Baynes copyright © C.S. Lewis Pte. Ltd., from *The Lion, the Witch and the Wardrobe* by C.S. Lewis, copyright © C.S. Lewis Pte. Ltd., 1950 and *Prince Caspian*, copyright © C.S. Lewis Pte. Ltd., 1951. Reprinted by permission.

Front cover from *Stuart Little* by E.B. White, illustrated by Garth Williams (Puffin, 2000). Text copyright © E.B. White, 1973. Illustrations renewed copyright © Garth Williams, 1973.

Front cover from *Comet in Moominland* by Tove Jansson. Front cover illustration by Gerry Downes (Puffin 1967). Copyright © Tove Jansson. Back cover illustration from *Comet in Moominland* by Tove Jansson (Puffin, 1967). Illustration copyright © Gerry Downes.

Photographs

Camera Press 28; Hulton-Deutsch Collection/Corbis 15 (Fred Hollyer); Hulton-Getty Picture Collection Ltd 5, 19, 21, 23 (Haywood Magee), 24 (John Chillingworth), 26 & *cover* (Mpi Archives); Mary Evans Picture Library 7, 8 (Edwin Wallace), 10 & *cover*, 16 (Reginald Haines); Topham Picturepoint 12 & *cover*, 19.

All possible care has been taken to trace the ownership of each poem included in this selection and to obtain copyright permission for its use. If there are any omissions or if any errors have occurred, they will be corrected in subsequent editions, on notification to the Publishers.

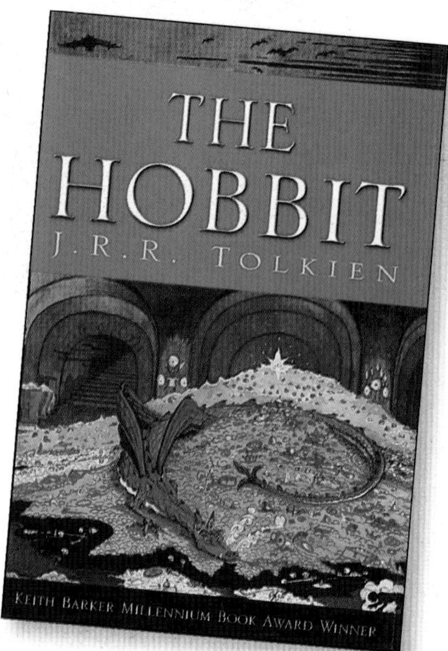

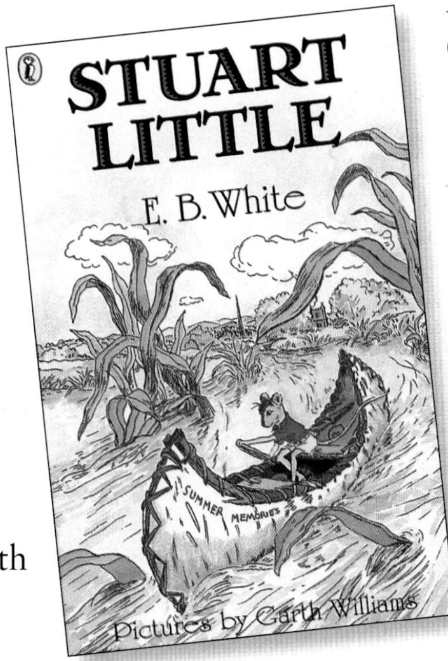

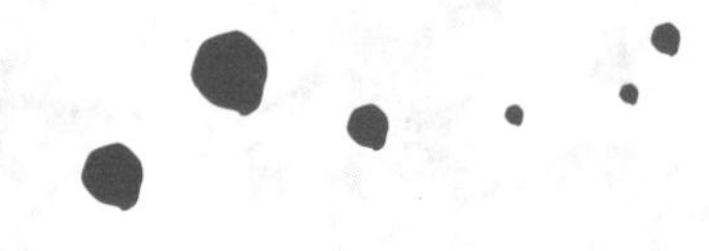